BEGINNING PIANO SOLO

GREAT TV THEMES

ISBN 978-1-5400-6749-4

Visit Hal Leonard Online at
www.halleonard.com

Contact us:
Hal Leonard
7777 West Bluemound Road
Milwaukee, WI 53213
Email: info@halleonard.com

In Europe, contact:
Hal Leonard Europe Limited
42 Wigmore Street
Marylebone, London, W1U 2RN
Email: info@halleonardeurope.com

In Australia, contact:
Hal Leonard Australia Pty. Ltd.
4 Lentara Court
Cheltenham, Victoria, 3192 Australia
Email: info@halleonard.com.au

CONTENTS

ADDAMS FAMILY THEME

Theme from the TV Show and Movie

Music and Lyrics by
VIC MIZZY

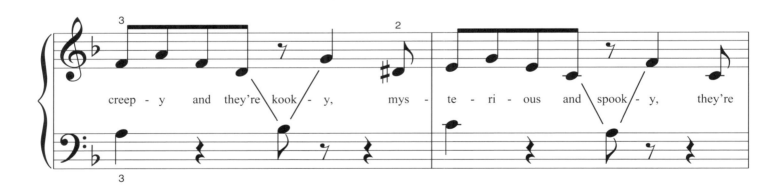

creep-y and they're kook-y, mys-te-ri-ous and spook-y, they're

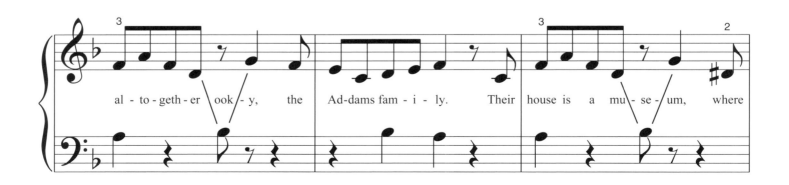

al-to-geth-er ook-y, the Ad-dams fam-i-ly. Their house is a mu-se-um, where

peo - ple come to see 'em, they real - ly are a scree -um, the Ad-dams fam - i - ly.

(Spoken:) Neat.   *Sweet.*

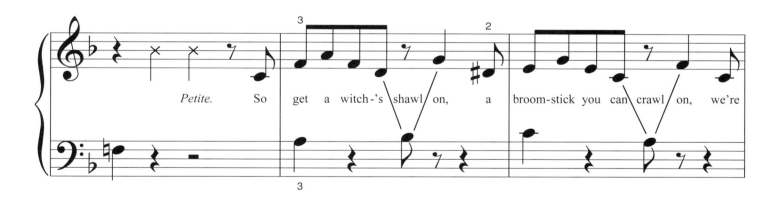

Petite.   So get a witch-'s shawl on, a broom-stick you can crawl on, we're

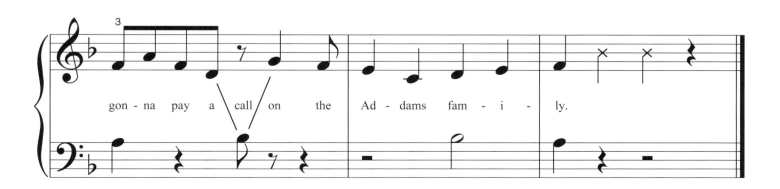

gon - na pay a call on the Ad - dams fam - i - ly.

ARTHUR THEME
from the TV series ARTHUR

Words and Music by JUDITH HENDERSON
and JERMEY DEVILLIERS

Ev - 'ry day when you're walk - in' down ___ the street, ___ ev - 'ry-

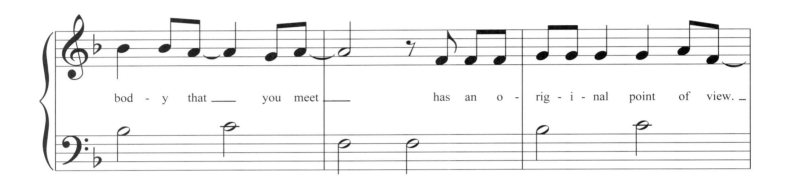

bod - y that ___ you meet ___ has an o - rig - i - nal point of view. ___

And I say hey! What a

won - der - ful kind of day when we can learn to work ___ and play ___

7

To Coda ⊕

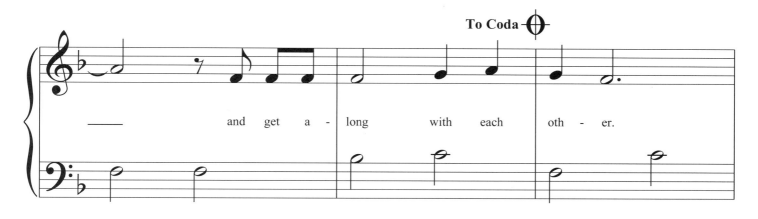

___ and get a - long with each oth - er.

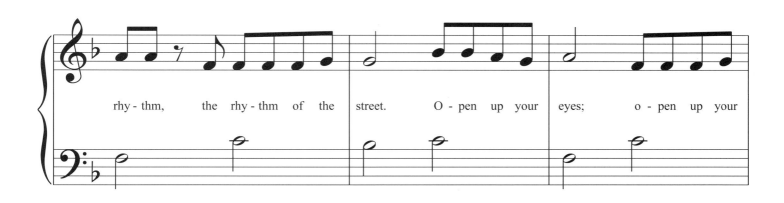

You got - ta lis - ten to your heart, lis - ten to the beat, lis - ten to the

rhy - thm, the rhy - thm of the street. O - pen up your eyes; o - pen up your

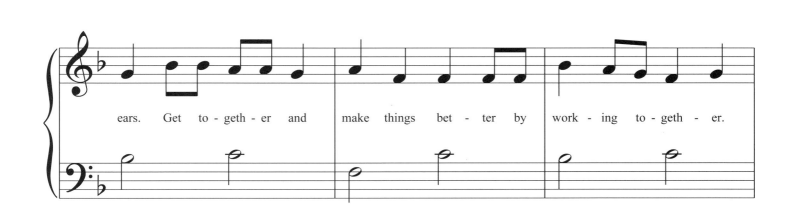

ears. Get to - geth - er and make things bet - ter by work - ing to - geth - er.

It's a sim - ple mes - sage and it comes from the

heart: __ Be - lieve in your self, for that's the place to start. __

D.S. al Coda

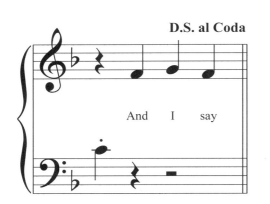

And I say

CODA

oth - er. Hey! What a won - der - ful kind of

day. Hey! What a won - der - ful kind of day. Hey!

DORA THE EXPLORER THEME SONG

from DORA THE EXPLORER

Words and Music by JOSH SITRON,
SARAH DURKEE and WILLIAM STRAUS

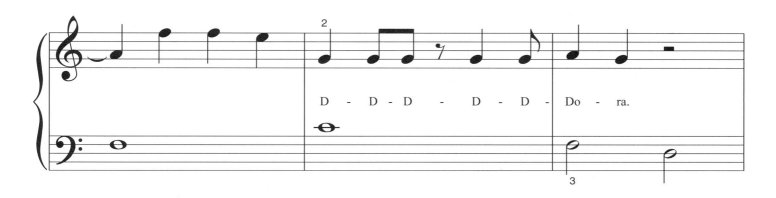

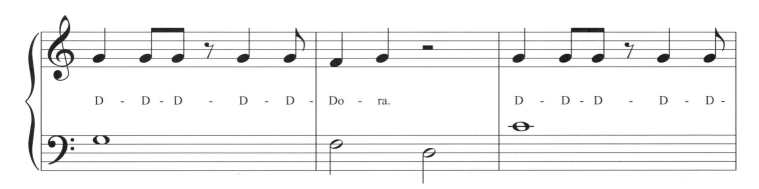

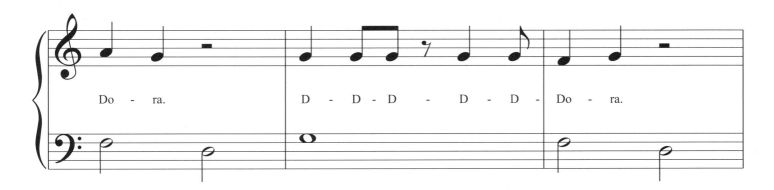

Do - ra, Do - ra, Do - ra the Ex - plor - er.

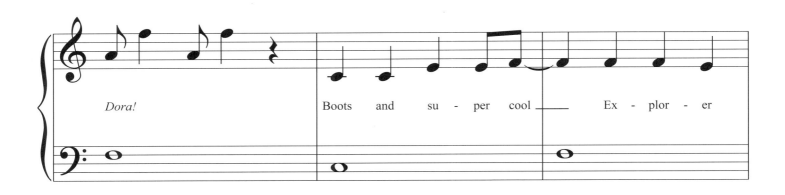

Dora! Boots and su - per cool ___ Ex - plor - er

Do - ra. *(We need your help.)* *(Grab your backpack!)*

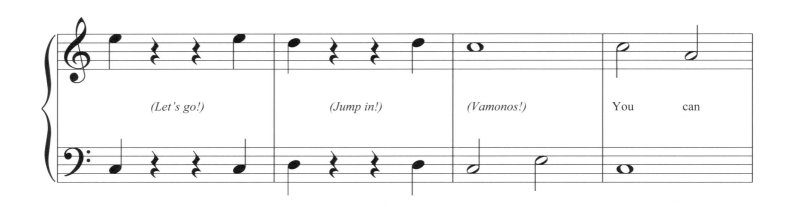

(Let's go!) *(Jump in!)* *(Vamonos!)* You can

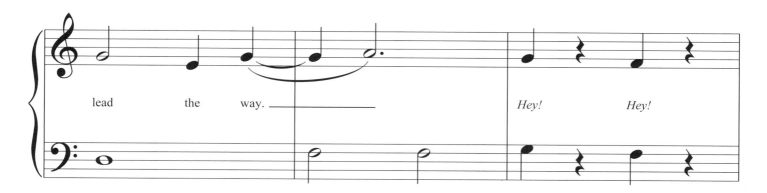

lead the way.   *Hey!*   *Hey!*

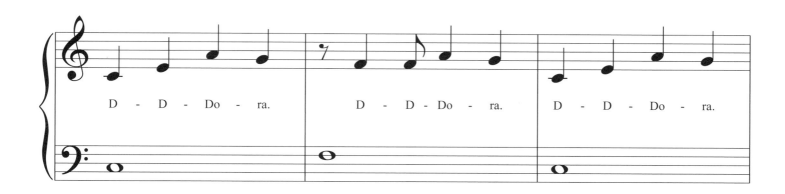

D - D - Do - ra.   D - D - Do - ra.   D - D - Do - ra.

D - D - Do - ra.

Do - ra the Ex - plor - er!

BOSS OF ME
(Theme from MALCOLM IN THE MIDDLE)

By JOHN FLANSBURGH
and JOHN LINNELL

Moderately fast Rock

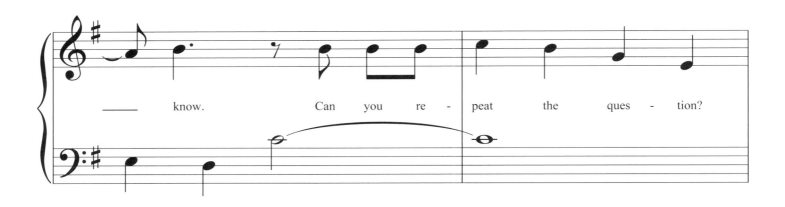

You're not the boss of me ____ now, and you're not so big.

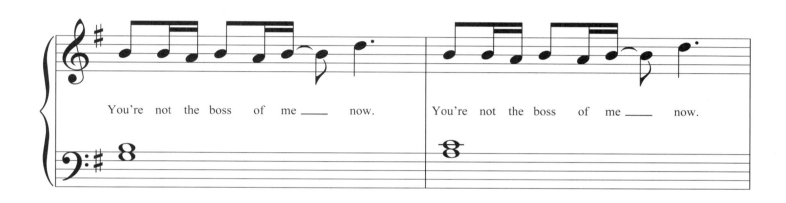

You're not the boss of me ____ now. You're not the boss of me ____ now.

You're not the boss of me ____ now, and you're not so big.

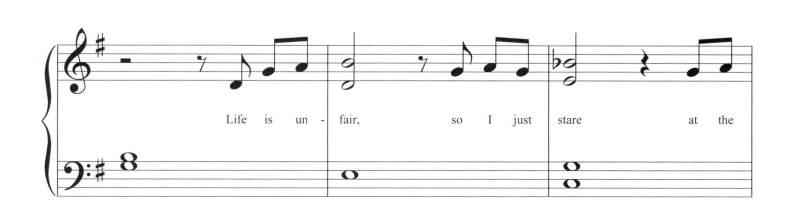

Life is un - fair, so I just stare at the

14

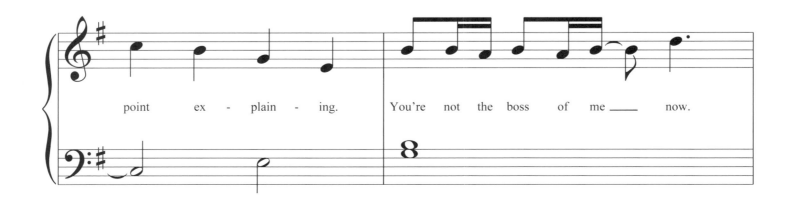

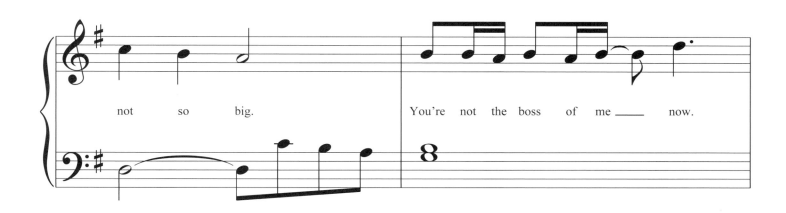

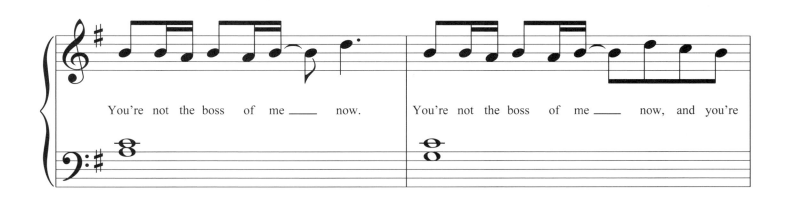

Slower, freely

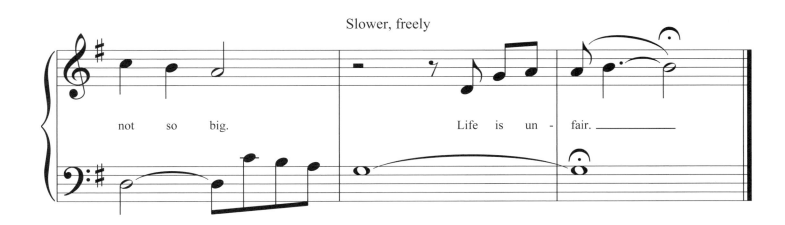

HAWAII FIVE-O THEME

from the Television Series

By MORT STEVENS

With a driving beat

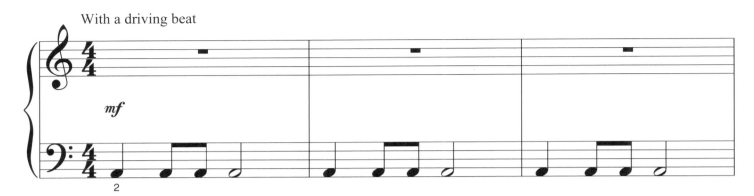

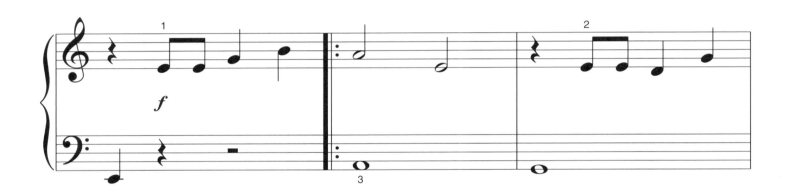

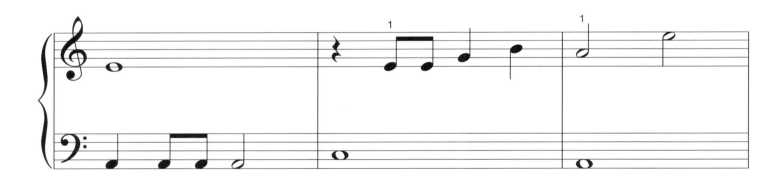

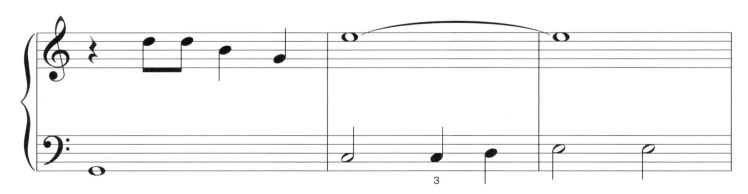

JEOPARDY THEME
from the Television Game Show

Music by MERV GRIFFIN

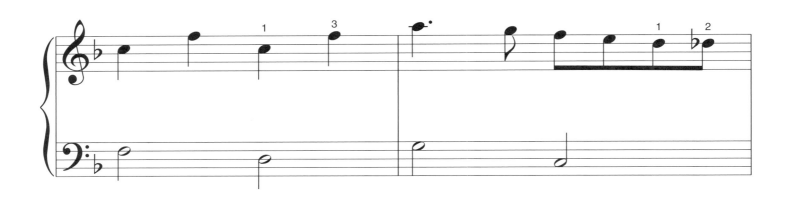

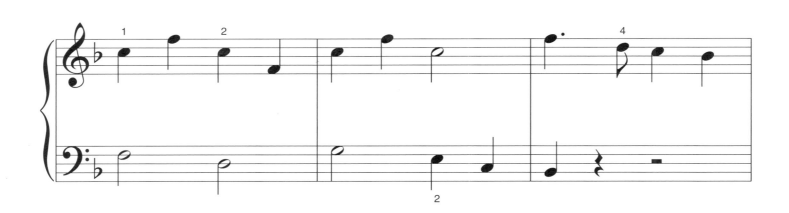

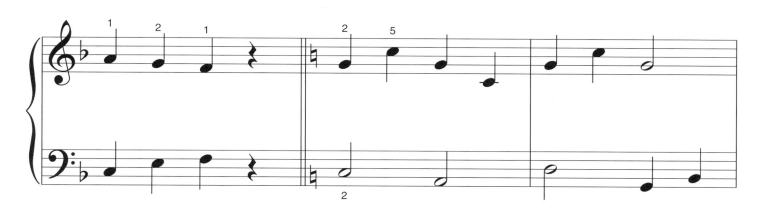

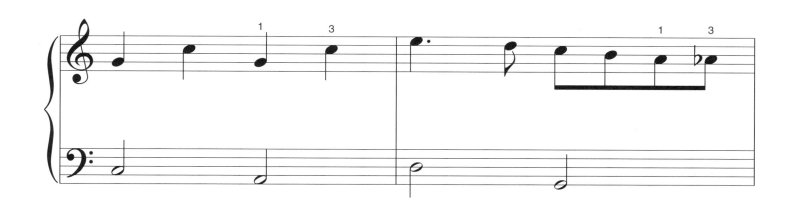

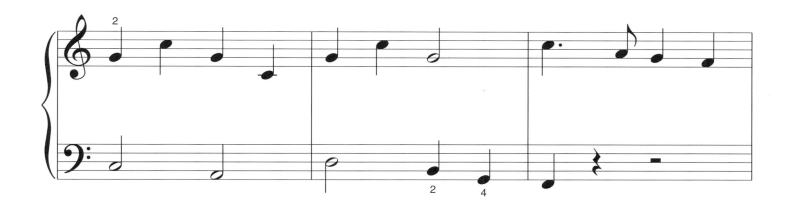

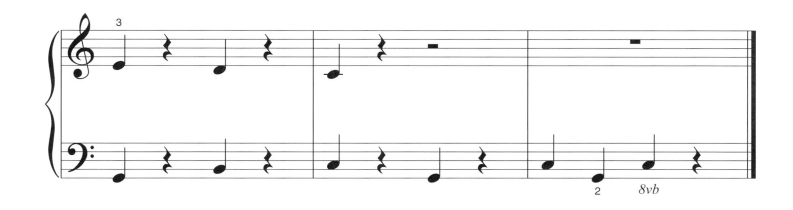

MISSION: IMPOSSIBLE THEME

from the Paramount Television Series MISSION: IMPOSSIBLE

By LALO SCHIFRIN

Moderately

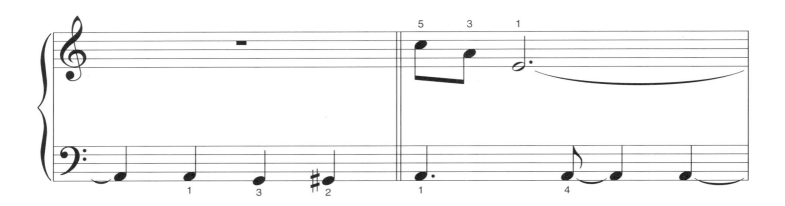

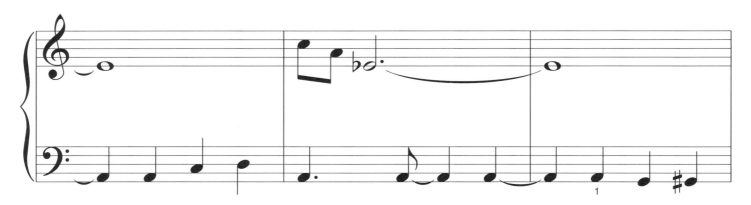

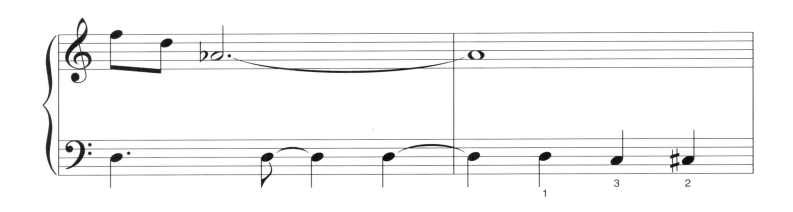

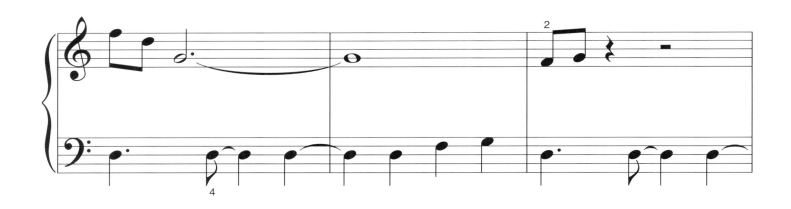

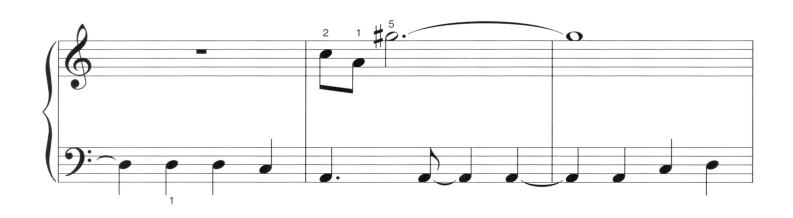

SESAME STREET THEME

from the Television Series SESAME STREET

Words by BRUCE HART,
JON STONE and JOE RAPOSO
Music by JOE RAPOSO

Sun - ny
Come and

day, sweep - in' the clouds a - way.
play! Ev - 'ry - thing's A - O. - K.

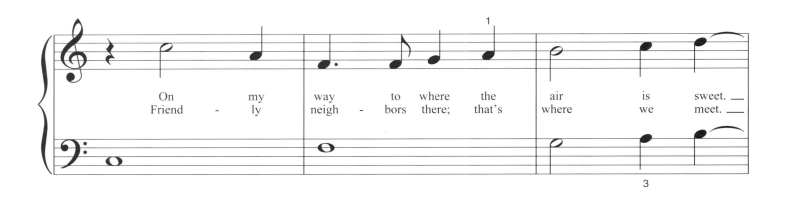

On my way to where the air is sweet. __
Friend - ly neigh - bors there; that's where we meet. __

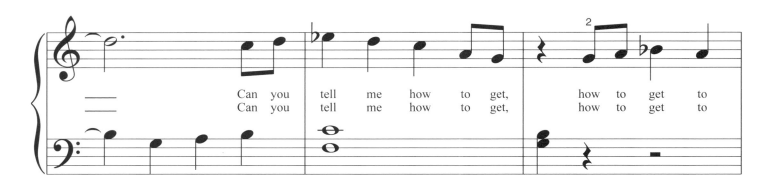

__ Can you tell me how to get, how to get to
__ Can you tell me how to get, how to get to

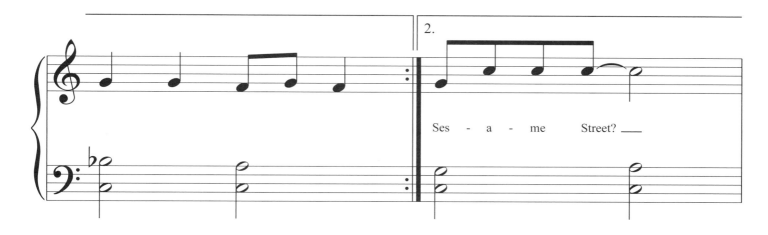

WON'T YOU BE MY NEIGHBOR?

(It's a Beautiful Day in the Neighborhood)

from MISTER ROGERS' NEIGHBORHOOD

Words and Music by
FRED ROGERS

It's a beau - ti - ful day in this neigh - bor - hood, a
neigh - bor - ly day in this beau - ty - wood, a

beau - ti - ful day for a neigh - bor. Would you be mine? Could you
neigh - bor - ly day for a beau - ty. Would you be mine? Could you

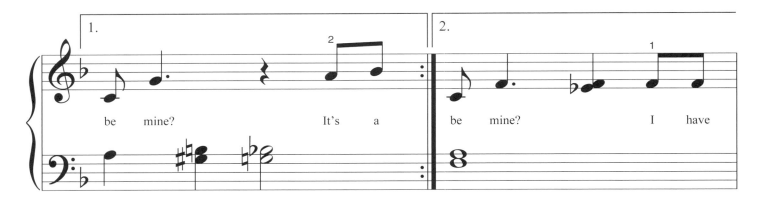

be mine? It's a
be mine? I have

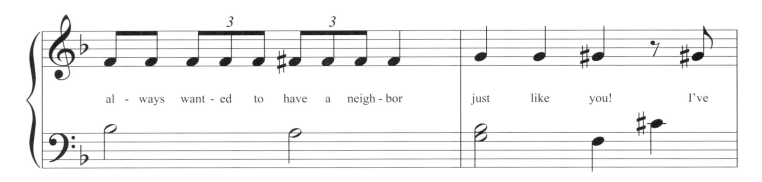

al - ways want - ed to have a neigh - bor just like you! I've

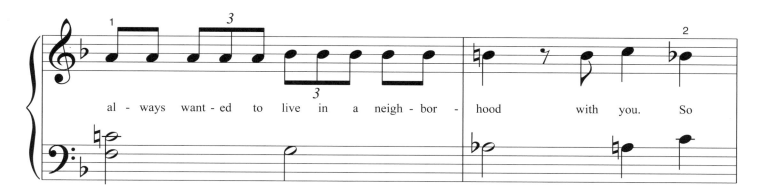

al - ways want - ed to live in a neigh - bor - hood with you. So

let's make the most of this beau - ti - ful day, since we're to - geth - er we might as well say,

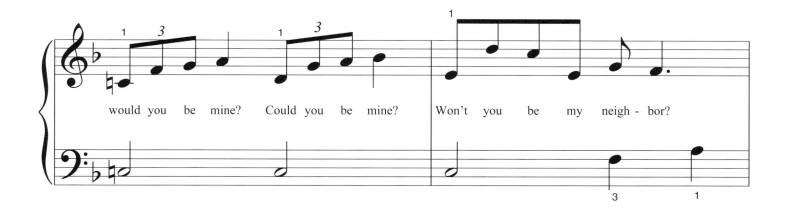

would you be mine? Could you be mine? Won't you be my neigh - bor?

Slower

Won't you please, won't you please? Please won't you be my neigh - bor?

NFL ON FOX THEME

from the Fox Sports Broadcasts of THE NFL ON FOX

By PHIL GARROD,
REED HAYS and SCOTT SCHREER

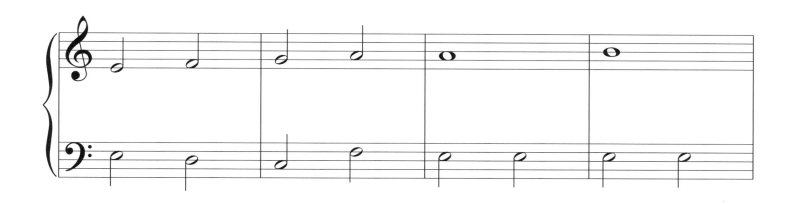

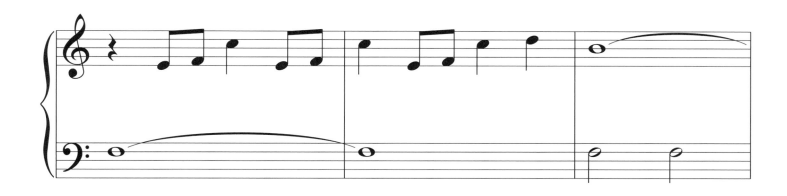

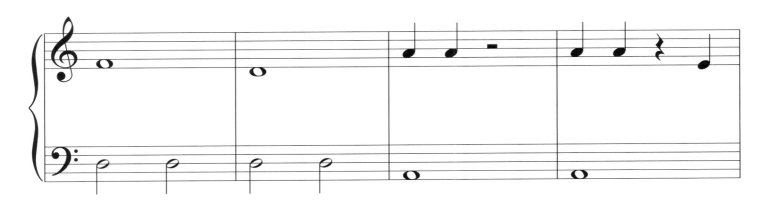

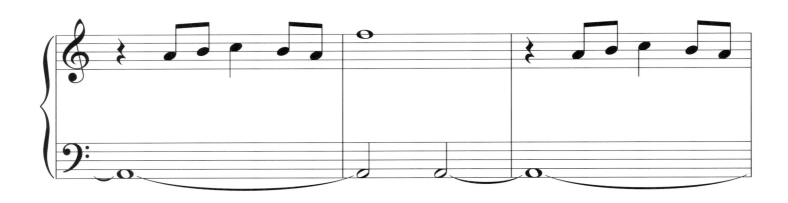

BEGINNING PIANO SOLO

Hal Leonard Beginning Piano Solos are created for students in the first and second years of study. These arrangements include a simple presentation of melody and harmony for a first "solo" experience. See www.halleonard.com for complete song lists.

00153652 **The Charlie Brown Collection™** $10.99

00316058 **First Book of Disney Solos** $12.99

00311065 **Jazz Standards** $9.95

00103239 **The Phantom of the Opera** $12.99

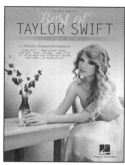

00175650 **Best of Taylor Swift**... $12.99

00156395 **Adele** $12.99

00311063 **Classical Favorites** $8.99

00130375 **Frozen** $12.99

00118420 **Best of Carole King** ... $10.99

00175142 **Pop Hits** $10.99

00119401 **Tangled** $10.99

00306568 **The Beatles** $12.99

00316082 **Contemporary Disney Solos** $12.99

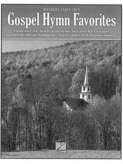

00311799 **Gospel Hymn Favorites** $8.99

00103351 **Les Misérables** $12.99

00311271 **Praise & Worship Favorites** $9.95

00110390 **10 Fun Favorites** $9.99

00307153 **Songs of the Beatles** $9.99

00311431 **Disney Classics** $10.99

00311064 **Greatest Pop Hits** $9.99

00319465 **The Lion King** $12.99

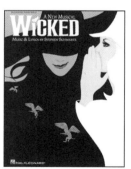

00316037 **The Sound of Music** ... $10.99

00109365 **Wicked** $10.99

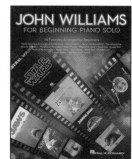

00279152 **Cartoon Favorites** $9.99

00264691 **Disney Hits** $10.99

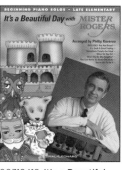

00319418 **It's a Beautiful Day with Mr. Rogers** $8.99

00110402 **The Most Beautiful Songs Ever** $14.99

00110287 **Star Wars** .. $12.99

00194545 **John Williams** $10.99

HAL•LEONARD®
www.halleonard.com

Prices, contents and availability are subject to change without notice. Disney characters and artwork TM & © 2019 Disney

FIRST 50

You've been taking lessons, you've got a few chords under your belt, and you're ready to buy a songbook. Now what? Hal Leonard has the answers in its *First 50* series.

These books contain easy to intermediate arrangements with lyrics for must-know songs.
Each arrangement is simple and streamlined, yet still captures the essence of the tune.

First 50 Acoustic Songs You Should Play on Piano
00293416 Easy Piano.........................$16.99

First 50 Baroque Pieces You Should Play on Piano
00291453 Easy Piano.........................$14.99

First 50 Songs by the Beatles You Should Play on the Piano
00172236 Easy Piano......................$19.99

First 50 Broadway Songs You Should Play on the Piano
00150167 Easy Piano.........................$14.99

First 50 Christmas Carols You Should Play on the Piano
00147216 Easy Piano.........................$14.99

First 50 Christmas Songs You Should Play on the Piano
00172041 Easy Piano.........................$14.99

First 50 Classic Rock Songs You Should Play on Piano
00195619 Easy Piano.........................$16.99

First 50 Classical Pieces You Should Play on the Piano
00131436 Easy Piano Solo................$14.99

First 50 Country Songs You Should Play on the Piano
00150166 Easy Piano.........................$14.99

First 50 Disney Songs You Should Play on the Piano
00274938 Easy Piano.........................$16.99

First 50 Early Rock Songs You Should Play on the Piano
00160570 Easy Piano.........................$14.99

First 50 Folk Songs You Should Play on the Piano
00235867 Easy Piano.........................$14.99

First 50 4-Chord Songs You Should Play on the Piano
00249562 Easy Piano.........................$16.99

First 50 Gospel Songs You Should Play on Piano
00282526 Easy Piano.........................$14.99

First 50 Hymns You Should Play on Piano
00275199 Easy Piano.........................$14.99

First 50 Jazz Standards You Should Play on Piano
00196269 Easy Piano.........................$14.99

First 50 Kids' Songs You Should Play on Piano
00196071 Easy Piano.........................$14.99

First 50 Latin Songs You Should Play on the Piano
00248747 Easy Piano.........................$16.99

First 50 Movie Songs You Should Play on the Piano
00150165 Easy Piano.........................$16.99

First 50 Movie Themes You Should Play on Piano
00278368 Easy Piano.........................$16.99

First 50 Songs You Should Play on the Organ
00288203 ....$19.99

First 50 Piano Duets You Should Play
00276571 1 Piano, 4 Hands...............$19.99

First 50 Pop Ballads You Should Play on the Piano
00248987 Easy Piano.........................$16.99

First 50 Pop Hits You Should Play on the Piano
00234374 Easy Piano.........................$16.99

First 50 Popular Songs You Should Play on the Piano
00131140 Easy Piano.........................$16.99

First 50 R&B Songs You Should Play on Piano
00196028 Easy Piano.........................$14.99

First 50 3-Chord Songs You Should Play on Piano
00249666 Easy Piano.........................$16.99

First 50 Worship Songs You Should Play on Piano
00287138 Easy Piano.........................$16.99

HAL•LEONARD®

www.halleonard.com

Prices, content and availability subject to change without notice.